The Psychology of Porn:
Essays on Pornography
Objectification & Healing

Andrew J. Bauman

DEDICATION

To the men and women who have suffered silently in shame and self-hatred due to objectification and pornography. May we deeply drink from the cup of liberation.

CONTENTS

ACKNOWLEDGMENTS

First of all I want to thank my wife, Christy. She has taught me so much that is within this book. My dear, we have suffered together to learn these heartbreaking truths. Thank you for your love and your belief in my goodness, it has transformed me. May I continue to become the man you knew I was when we married. Thank you to my editor, Rose Jackson who labored over these words to make it something beautiful.

INTRODUCTION

BLESSING PORNOGRAPHY:
A NEW APPROACH TO RECOVERY

Christian Newswire reported that 68% of Christian men and 50% of pastors confessed to viewing porn weekly. That is nearly 7 out of 10 Christian men, and half of all evangelical pastors! Porn has been shown to ruin marriages and contribute to loss of jobs, severe depression, and sexual issues within committed relationships. The intention of this essay is not to convince you that porn is an epidemic or even a problem—that's easy, just look at the statistics and the countless shattered lives. The purpose of this essay is to ask you to look more deeply into the desire and beauty behind the darkness of pornography and take the courageous step of blessing. Let me explain by sharing some of my story.

I come from the first generation where pornography invaded our sacred spaces. I was 12 when my family first got dial-up Internet in my home. My friend Steve was a grand teacher; he showed me how to search for naked women and erase the history so our parents wouldn't find out. We knew how to use the computer better than our parents did, and this new, uncharted, nude world was before us. It was always accessible, simple, and incredibly exhilarating. We did not need be afraid of getting caught; we became masters of deception and internalized our shame.

From 12 to 25 years of age, I was addicted to porn. At times I had long seasons of sobriety, I had accountability partners and groups I attended. (In one particular church group we formed a "jackpot," where if you masturbated you owed the pot $5—we all donated a lot of money.) I prayed 10,000 times for God to remove temptation, for God to forgive me, or at least show me mercy and make me a eunuch. Nothing worked, God remained silent, and I could never bring myself to the knife. My computer screen remained lit, I still liked naked women, and shame bound me.

For nearly 13 years I tried to humiliate and hate myself into transformation. It didn't work. I thought if I abused myself enough, I could somehow forgive my sins (God forgives sins better than I do), or wash away how I had objectified and harmed all those storyless women. The more shame, the more contempt, the deeper into addiction I went; shame and contempt always lead to greater darkness and entrapment. I despised myself for what I was doing and believed I deserved the death I was heaping onto myself. There was no amount of penance that could fit my crimes.

Bound by shame is exactly where the Thief wanted me. I was immobilized, the feeling of running full speed in 3 feet of water—I was getting nowhere fast. Evil had stolen from me and was not going to stop until I was killed and destroyed. As Dr. Allender puts it, "Evil steals innocence and joy. It hates our potential intimacy with God, therefore it uses the desire God created in us for beauty, sensuality, and the hunger for wisdom to seduce us away from God." Evil was seductive and turned me against myself and my holy desire for beauty.

To begin to break the curse that pornography had over my life, I had to come to the place of blessing, or the addiction and agreement with Evil could not be broken. Yet how do you bless something that is so fundamentally wrong? The naked body is not evil—it's actually quite good and stunning, good enough for it to bear God's image and house God's spirit. We enter into the realm of evil when we objectify and deface the image of God in another. For me, to begin to heal I had to come to see that porn was actually the closest thing to heaven I could access at the time. I had to come to the place of blessing, or the addiction and agreement with Evil could not be broken.

My family devastated by divorce, infidelity, and addiction; my father not present and silent, my mother nearby yet so far away, I longed for any beauty in the desolation of my life. I longed to be touched, to be held, to feel pleasure, and to numb my pain. This was the pain behind my porn use. I tried drugs, I tried alcohol, but nothing quite touched my desire and broken heart like Eve's body. As John Eldredge writes, "Eve is the crescendo, the final, astonishing work of God. Woman. In one last flourish creation comes to a finish not with Adam, but with *Eve*. She is the Master's finishing touch." Once I realized that beauty and desire were not the problem, but my perversion of them was, I could begin to disrupt Evil's hold over me.

There is no place in this world where I see more of Evil's distortion of goodness and beauty than within pornography. The crown of creation objectified into oblivion. The kingdom of darkness twists what is holy into something sinister. Evil is a master deceiver and father of lies (John 8:44). My desire for beauty and sensuality was fundamentally good and holy, and I needed to bless that to become free. The orphan within me needed unconditional love and delight, and the false intimacy of pornography offered me comfort and met those desires where my parents could not. In many ways pornography was a good parent (and equally a destructive one). Until you can name the goodness of what your addiction gave/gives you, you cannot let go of the devastating cycle.

When I began to engage my story with radical kindness, I could finally enter into authentic repentance and let go of the addiction that was destroying my life. Only now am I able to comprehend Roman 2:4, "God's kindness is meant to lead you to repentance." Only through the kindness of God have I been able to enter heartache, grief, forgiveness, and what it means to recover from the brokenness of my sexuality.

This radical embrace to self-kindness is part of the new approach to pornography recovery we must embrace. Recovering from compulsive pornography use is not a tranquil or relaxed journey. We can effortlessly drift into regular pornography use, but we must be deliberate and intentional when we choose to walk away from it. Just trying harder, i.e. "white knuckling" never works. The typical religious approaches to recovery have not been helpful, but more of glorified behavioral management. Shaming ourselves over and over to pay penance for our transgressions doesn't work. Many times prayers to stop seem to work for a few days until we find ourselves in the same spot, unable to resist our compulsive sexual behaviors. Self-contempt and self-hatred won't remedy the late night cravings. We need a deeper engagement with our understanding of pornography and how to stop our addiction to it. So how do we reclaim what we have lost to pornography? How can we stop this behavior from controlling our lives? The truth is if we can look beneath pornography and see it for what it truly is we can begin the process of maturation, out of dependence and into sexually healthy adults.

Here are a few questions this book will address:

- How can I stop?
- How can I respect myself again?
- How do I stop when part of me wants to indulge and another part desperately doesn't?
- Is there hope for me?
- Can I have a normal relationship again?
- I want to honor women, but how?

If you find yourself in the tension of these questions, of not wanting to continue your current relationship with pornography and wanting a new approach to quitting, this book of essays is for you. It is important to note a few core assumptions I am making as I write this book.

1) You are good.

Even if you are involved in deep deception, participating in a hidden life, there is a goodness to you, of which you have lost sight. Just because your choices with your addiction are poor does not make you bad. Guilt is an appropriate emotion to feel when you are participating in something harmful and damaging; shame is a dicey emotion that confuses your guilt for your behavior into a condemnation of self. You are not bad, there is hope for your transformation.

2) A spiritual lens

I come to this conversation with a spiritual lens. I am a Christian, I believe in the role and presence of God and the role of the Evil one in our addictive journey. God is truth; the more we live in truth the more we experience God. Our pilgrimage to become more honest and authentic human beings is a journey to know God more fully. Truth always leads to some type of redemptive death that blazes a trail of liberation, and it is worth every drop of blood shed along that painful path toward freedom. When we live in truth, we defeat the roots of addiction, shame, self-contempt, and the full arsenal that Evil uses to kill, steal, and destroy (John 10:10). What is the reward for living in truth? It is as simple and as complex as access to the Most High. God is truth. Our engagement with truth is at the core of knowing God. All liberation is rooted in the God who guides us there. What if each time we courageously entered the truth of our stories we were drawn into perfect, intimate communion with our creator? We must look at authenticity through this celestial lens knowing that resurrection cannot co-exist with what remains hidden within ourselves.

3) We are all addicts.

We are all addicted to something. Work, praise, food, sex, our smart phones, we all seek escape from pain through a variety of ways. Porn is just one of those ways, and the one you have chosen. Own it, own your own dependence and problem with porn. Many folks have a difficult time with the term, porn addict, as if the label is some type of final nail in the coffin of your shame. I think admitting that you have an unhealthy relationship with pornography is the beginning of letting it go, and naming that you are an addict can be helpful. It is not who you are, but what you have done. You have the power to change your relationship with porn.

4) It's never too late to change, but be patient.

Many people begin the healing process when they are caught, when their marriage is crumbling, or when they realize they don't know how to keep a genuine, long lasting, intimate relationship with a real human. No matter how long you have been living a secret life, it's never too late to change. Whether you have been addicted to pornography for 3 weeks or 3 decades, the good news is that you can still transform your life.

The bad new is that recovery will be difficult, it has to be, for it to be real, it's difficult to trust anything that comes too easily, including your healing. Let's say you have been addicted to porn for 20 years. From the ages of 12 to 32, it started with curiosity and slowly turned into regular use multiple times a week. Let's be conservative in our estimate and say you have looked twice a week for the last 20 years. 52 weeks in a year comes to 104 instances of looking at porn any given year. 104 times a year x 20 minutes of partaking = 2,080 instances of looking at porn in your lifetime. 2,080 instances of looking at porn x 20 minutes each = 41,600 minutes during your life, which means nearly 700 hours of your life! Which is nearly 30 days; an entire month of your life has been lived behind the screen peering at naked women! You don't think this has an impact on your brain? Or the way you do life? 20 years of immersing yourself in anything will take a long time to undo. So please be patient. I have many clients that work hard for a few months and think they should be further along than they are.

Change takes time and patience. This journey of recovery will take no less than a year of full commitment to your sobriety but many times can take many years until you are mature enough to outgrow your relationship to pornography, and choose the healthier path of relating.

RELATIONSHIPS

A PORNOGRAPHIC STYLE OF RELATING

I come from the first generation where Internet pornography entered our homes with devastating regularity. The pattern of pornography use has shown no sign of slowing down. As Belinda Luscombe writes in her *Time* article "Porn and the Threat to Vitality," an independent Web-tracking company totaled the number of U.S. visitors to porn sites at around 58 million monthly in February 2006. Then, "Ten years later…the number was 107 million." That is 107 million visitors a month in the U.S. alone!

This amount of consumption, along with the church's notorious silence around the topic of sexuality, has distorted my own sexual development and that of millions of young men and women who grew up immersed in a pornified society. The consequences have been dire and are just starting to come to the surface, as addicted millennials have begun to marry and attempt to attain healthy relationships.

One of the chief consequences is the development of a **Pornographic Style of Relating (PSR).** This style of relating is most learned when pornography becomes your primary teacher or guide in your sexual development. We learn certain ways of being, and then those ways are unconsciously lived out in relationship. I will briefly discuss six ways of living out of a PSR, and examine what those categories look like when they are restored in healthy relationship. This style of relating is most learned when pornography is your primary teacher or guide in your sexual development.

The first category of a Pornographic Style of Relating is that of **control**—rooted in being the only one in the dynamic, which is a non-mutual relationship alone with imagery. When you are by yourself masturbating to images, there is no one else to satisfy, no one else to consider, and you get to control the entire scene. The set-up, the romance, the rituals, the climax are in your power. This creates an innate selfishness and an unconscious desire for absolute control over intimate relationship. In a redeemed sexuality, this category is that of **freedom**, rooted in a maturity and security of both partners, allowing each to choose to come and go and know the inherent goodness of the other.

The second category of a Pornographic Style of Relating is **objectification**. The addict, over the years, is looking at thousands upon thousands of images; those bodies become seared into our brains over time, and we become desensitized (Kühn, Simone & Gallinat, 2014). Research has also revealed that "our brain's dopamine receptors shrink in response to chronic overstimulation" (Kenny, Voren & Johnson, 2013). In pornography, the unknown bodies have no names or stories and have become means to an end, serving only the purpose of attaining orgasm. After they no longer serve a purpose, they are cheaply discarded. This pornographic development leads to dehumanizing sexual behavior and non-positive views of women (Bridges, 2010), and causes those with PSR to chronically jump from relationship to relationship (just like clicking from pornographic image to pornographic image), looking for perfection and completion to be found in a person.

This category of objectification restored becomes the category of **honor**. The partner is respected for their entire being; their voice, opinions, preferences all matter, and equal weight is given to both parties. When the *imago Dei* is recognized in the face of the other, honor is sure to follow.

The third category of a Pornographic Style of Relating is **speed**. The rapid pace of relationships comes to resemble the quick climax of intensity around pornography, the rush and thrill of not getting exposed, an urgency for consummation, and ultimately an abrupt and inevitable ending (normally with shame attached). These traits are opposite to sustaining long-lasting intimacy. The speed of relationship normally involves high emotional and sexual linking without the proper time to grow together deeply, and other areas of relationship such as intellectual and spiritual connections are neglected or completely forgotten.

The redeemed trait of this category is **gradual**—a slow build. A strong foundation of balanced intimacy, growth, tears, laughter, pain, and joy shared together. You grow in love, not accidentally fall in it. These are the things your grandmother taught you, and they could not be more true—or in more opposition to a PSR.

The fourth category of a Pornographic Style of Relating is **hunger**. There is a frantic need that must be filled by the other. This cavernous need consumes and devours both partners in an attempt to mend something broken inside. This category shows itself in co-dependent relationships, where both parties become enmeshed and no individuation can be found. The hunger drives them to consume—rather than delight in—the other.

This category of hunger redeemed is **desire**. Desire is a healthy longing and genuine want of the whole other, not a desperation to fulfill. A litmus test you can try when considering a relationship or when you want to know if you are acting out a PSR would be to recite this sentence, "I want you, but I do not need you to be okay." If you can confidently say that you will be hurt and disappointed, but ultimately "okay" without the other, you are living out of desire and not misguided famine. At that point they no longer define who you are but only what you long for. Opening your heart to another is an invitation to the real you, what you simultaneously most fear and most long to attain.

The fifth category of a Pornographic Style of Relating is **isolation**. We learn our sexuality behind closed doors, and in the dim light of the computer screen our sexuality remains hidden, even from ourselves. We come to protect this isolation as some type of sacred space, and even the thought of inviting another human in feels threatening and disruptive. The isolation fuels the secret life and separates us from the loving relationships that we most need.

Redeemed isolation is the category of **communion**. This communion is a shared open bond with another person, vulnerably allowing the other into the most guarded territory of your sexuality. Opening your heart to another is an invitation to the real you, what you simultaneously most fear and most long to attain.

The sixth and final category is that of **fantasy**. Fantasy is an escape from what is real. Whether it be difficult emotions, such as stress, anxiety, depression, or just the pain that genuine relationship inevitably brings, fantasy relieves those struggles for a moment. While healthy relationships live in the truth, pornography helps bolster a life of fantasy that is difficult to undo. Fantasy brings relief but does not bring restoration.

The redeemed counterpart to this category is **authenticity**. For relationships to remain thriving and true, both partners must be committed to voicing complaints, hopes, and desires, and living into what is most true. When one partner is still living out of a PSR, there is little to no chance that the couple can tackle what needs to addressed in the relationship.

My hope is that, whether you yourself are an addict or you are attempting to be in relationship with one, these categories can bring awareness and empower you toward action, ultimately owning your part in how you relate to the world and beginning the process of transformation that you were meant for.

References

Bridges, A (2010). "Pornography's Effects on Interpersonal Relationships," in The Social Costs of Pornography, edited by James R. Stoner Jr. and Donna M. Hughes, 89–110. Princeton, New Jersey: Witherspoon Institute, 2010.

Kenny, Voren, and Johnson (2013). "Dopamine D2 Receptors and Striatopallidal Transmission in Addiction and Obesity." *Current Opinion in Neurobiology* 23, no. 4 (2013): 535–538.

Kühn, Simone and Gallinat (2014). "Brain Structure and Functional Connectivity Associated with Pornography Consumption: The Brain on Porn." *JAMA Psychiatry* (2014): 827–34.

Luscombe, B. (2016, March 31). Porn and the Threat to Virility. Retrieved September 20, 2016, from http://time.com/4277510/porn-and-the-threat-to-virility/

I, ANDREW, TAKE YOU, PORN, TO BE MY WIFE

Pornography use is not merely dependence, but intimate relationship. Giving up pornography is not like learning to eat less chocolate, or merely going to the gym more often, it's more like betraying a lover to whom you have been committed your entire adolescent and adult life. Not only a lover who YOU have been committed to but a lover who has been even more loyal TO YOU. Porn has always been there for you when no one else was. She soothed and rocked you when you were fearful. She held you when you were lonely; brought you relief when you were heartbroken. Porn has been so good to you. You feel indebted to her for how she has rescued you, the last thing you want is to leave such a sweet refuge and such a blameless lover.

But this sweet haven from harsh reality has now become your prison. Your vow to porn must be broken. This is one divorce that cannot come too soon but must come kindly. We must kindly disavow our commitment to porn, grieve its loss in our lives, and recommit to learning how to do relationship without dependence and obsession.

As you read the marriage ceremony to pornography below, what is evoked in you? Are you aware of how real your relational commitment is to porn? When did you make your vow? Is your relationship to porn something you are willing to grieve and release?

Andrew J. Bauman

The Marriage Vows to Pornography

Minister: "Porn, will you have this man to be your husband; to live together with him in the covenant of marriage? Will you love him, comfort him, honor and keep him, in sickness and in health; and, forsaking all others, be faithful unto him as long as you both shall live?"

Porn: "I will."

Minister: "Andrew, will you have porn to be your wife; to live together with her in the covenant of marriage? Will you love her, comfort her, honor and keep her, in sickness and in health; and, forsaking all others, be faithful unto her as long as you both shall live?"

Andrew: "I will."

Andrew faces Porn and takes her right hand in his, then says:

Andrew: "In the name of God, I, Andrew take you, Porn, to be my wife, to have and to hold from this day forward, for better, for worse, for richer, for poorer, in sickness and in health, to love and to cherish, until we are parted by death. This is my solemn vow.

They drop hands. Porn then takes his right hand in hers, then says:

Porn: In the name of God, I, Porn, take you, Andrew, to be my husband, to have and to hold from this day forward, for better, for worse, for richer, for poorer, in sickness and in health, to love and to cherish, until we are parted by death. This is my solemn vow.

Disavowing Marriage to Pornography

Take deep breaths as you prepare to speak aloud. Whenever you are ready, read and ponder the new vow below. Let the words settle within you. After a few readings, will you prayerfully consider reciting the words below out loud with conviction, kindness, and authority?

Andrew: "In the name of God, I, Andrew, give myself permission to leave you, Porn. I first want to thank you for being there for me when others were not, for holding me for better, for worse, for richer, for poorer, in sickness and in health, and loving me until death. But now, since I am dying with you in my life, I must break my pledge to you. I must choose a non-addicted life, and grow apart from you. I will miss you, but I will no longer choose you. I bless you, and now I must say goodbye. I now release myself from my commitment to you."

A Few Clarifying Thoughts on the idea of "Blessing Pornography"

In response to possible confusion about the radical idea of "blessing pornography"; is not as one reader said, *"You are asking me to rejoice in pornography, you've asked me to rejoice in my abuser."* I would never bless the Evil that porn has brought to my life or the fact that it nearly killed me.

Masochism comes to mind if that were my stance. That would be sick, abusive, and reckless. But blessing your story (read Dan Allender's work on "blessing your story" and Robert Master's work on Emotional Intimacy) is not about "rejoicing in pornography". It is about kindness and becoming intimate with your own darkness. Romans 2:4 *"Can't you see that his kindness is intended to turn you from your sin?"* What does it mean to you to embody God's kindness towards your own sin? What I am trying to say is we change much more fully through blessing and kindness than through curse and contempt, which is what we normally show towards our sin. Blessing our failures and answering the question of how porn served us is important to the healing process.

PORNOGRAPHY & EMOTIONAL ENMESHMENT

The pattern I often see when helping others process an unwanted relationship with pornography is a correlation between addiction and the propensity toward emotionally enmeshed relationships. Pornography teaches us to relate with emotional fusion and an inability to differentiate in a healthy way (this is another aspect of Pornographic Style of Relating). This essay will help define what emotional enmeshment is, and if we find ourselves in this type of relationship, how we can move beyond this co-dependent style of relating.

What Is Emotional Enmeshment?

Ross Rosenberg's book, *The Human Magnet Syndrome: Why We Love People Who Hurt Us,* names a few indicators of an enmeshed relationship:

- "Neglecting other relationships because of obsession or concern about one relationship
- Happiness being contingent upon the relationship
- Self-esteem being contingent upon the relationship
- Feeling excessive anxiety, fear or a compulsion to fix the problem whenever there is a disagreement in the relationship

- A "feeling of loneliness pervading [your] psyche" when you are unable to be with the other person; this loneliness can "increase to the point of creating irrational desires to reconnect"

- Feeling a "symbiotic emotional connection"; in other words, if your partner is angry, upset or depressed, you become angry, upset, or depressed

- Feeling the overwhelming need to fix his/her situation and change his/her state of mind."

Just like pornography, there is an "all consuming" aspect to emotionally enmeshed relationships. There is an interlocking in which the two individuals become unrecognizable; you can no longer tell them apart. Feelings and emotions are dependent on those of the partner and no differentiation can be found.

Pornography and emotional enmeshment form a symbiotic relationship; both help reaffirm one's reliance on the other. As I have discussed in other essays, pornography creates the much-needed escape from internal pain, and porn can temporarily soothe our wounds with care and precision. This begins the process of eroticizing our deepest pain. In our deepest agonies, porn appears as a healer. This experience marks our psyche, creating an unconscious emotional enmeshment, dependence, and obsession with women which later presents as co-dependence within relationships.

For example, as a youngster, when my parents were splitting up and no one was talking about what was going on, I felt crazy inside. Nothing was being defined for me, and I had yet to develop a languaged emotional world.

Porn soothed, and then as I grew older real women served the same function for me. The adult addict unconsciously seeks wholeness from women; "*Soothe me, comfort my insecurities and fears, make me whole just like porn did!*", thus beginning the emotional enmeshed style of relating. As pornography moves from the origin point of genuine curiosity into darker forms of entrapment, obsession becomes a core part of the addictive process. Over time it manifests and devours our very being. As this entanglement grows stronger, the addict seeks needy women to enmesh with, and the dependence of a pornographic fix (using a woman inappropriately) becomes greater.

This obsessed way of being bleeds out into our everyday styles of relating and we begin to live from this gripped place. This could be considered the "creep factor", such as what you feel when observing a man stare unflinchingly at a woman as she walks by. This fixation becomes the fuel that drives the enmeshment. The addict thinks, "*If I only had her, she could make me happy, she could make me whole.*" His unconscious belief is that this woman has the power to mend an early childhood wound. Porn has soothed him so effectively in the moment that he comes to believe that a woman walking down the street can offer that same powerful relief. Even though the addict knows nothing about her, she may fit his pornographic fantasy structure, and like a charmed fairy-tale delusion, he believes they are meant to be together. He will obsess about her until enough time has passed or some life event snaps him back to reality. The addict then begins to scan his world until he transfers his fantasy onto someone else he unconsciously objectifies. This unhealthy pattern of moving from one fantasy target to another is part of the objectification of women and comes from a place of core wounding.

For us to end this unhealthy pattern of relating and begin to step into what it means to be relationally and sexual healthy, we must continue to have courage in the face of our fear and engage our pain that grows beneath the porn.

THE HEALTHY RELATIONSHIP INDICATOR

The graph below is what I call the healthy relationship indicator. It can be used as a measurement tool for therapists to measure couple's relational connectivity in a variety of places of intimacy. It can also be used to self rate to see where you and your partner are in your levels of relational connection, where you still need work, and where you are currently strong. This tool can be used to increase levels of communication and mature dialogue to help strengthen relationships.

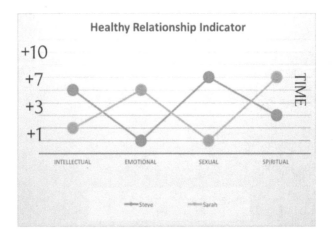

On the bottom of the graph are 4 common ways we connect. These are by no means the totality of how we relationally connect, just common and generalized themes to help locate where relationships can continue to grow in intimacy. To effectively use this for your own relationship, friends and/or for clients/patients you are working with towards growing their relational intimacy, all parties must be working with the same definitions of terms.

Define your terms of connection: What does it mean for you and your partner to connect intellectually? What books are you reading and discussing? What about the latest inspiring TED talk you watched? How are you and your partner engaging your minds together? What about your emotional connectivity? How do you both offer your vulnerabilities? How do you surrender control and power for the sake of being known? Do each of you speak of your feelings? Feelings are normally one word. I feel *sad*, I feel *happy*, I feel *stressed*, I feel *lonely*. Using what we feel as guideposts for connection with our partner. *It is important to note that emotional connection does not mean emotional co-dependence and/or emotional enmeshment (see essay on emotional enmeshment).* Emotional connection is about want and desire, not need and dependency.

It is also vital for you both to define sexual connection. Sexual connection is not just about frequency of sex, although that does factor into it, as many times there is a correlation between frequency and connection. But sexual connection is much more about the *intimacy and connection of the sexual encounters,* not just the intercourse or orgasm. Many times one partner will think they are very sexually connected to their partner while the other is feeling completely alone and unfulfilled in their sexuality. Do you hold eye connect while you have sex? Do you go slowly? Do you touch, massage, caress your partners body? Do you cuddle naked without intercourse? Can you be present with each other sexually without the pressure to always climax and orgasm? To be healthy sexually it means to "be fully with" the other, not "doing to" the other.

The last area of connection is that of spiritual intimacy. Do you connect deeply over your spirituality; e.g. prayer life or other spiritual disciplines, spiritual longings and practices? How do you and your partner connect spirituality? This is a place that many couples either completely ignore or completely indulge, forgetting that there is a balance needed with all the other forms of connectivity.

How to Use the Measurement Tool?

The above measurement tool is plotted for clients Steve & Sarah. They individually (apart from each other) mark where they think their connection is in the listed category. How intellectually connected do you feel towards your partner? How emotionally connected are you to your partner? What level are you sexually connected? Spiritually connected? Then draw a line to the connected dots. A healthy relationship should look closer to a straight line, where as a relationship of concern would be one that is more mountainous, with sharp highs and lows.

Over time healthy relationships grow with intimacy and intensity, rather than sharp spikes with not much time to develop or grow connection over time.

WOMEN

MY LOVE & HATE FOR WOMEN:
A RECOVERING SEX ADDICT'S AMBIVELANCE WITH FEMININITY

I love women and I hate them. I need a woman close by to survive, yet I can't have a woman too close. If she gets too close, I will either self-destruct or annihilate her in a variety of socially acceptable, manipulative, systemic ways, like a brain surgeon using a scalpel. I have way too much power, and way too much fear to use my blade appropriately. This is the internal conflict for many men who struggle with sexual addiction.

The goal for men who are engaging in the dark side of our sexual addictions is first naming how we have disastrously botched our relationship with the feminine. Once we own our marred relationship to the feminine we can begin to step towards reclaiming what has been lost and courageously pursuing healthy relationships with women; honoring beauty rather than attempting to devour it. Though many men and women suffer from compulsive sexual behavior, I will be using stereotypical gender roles in referring to a male's addiction and its impact on his relationships, particularly with women.

An insecure woman who is full of self-contempt for her body and/or at war with her own gender is the *unconscious* perfect target for the insecure addict. (*I use the word unconscious because I truly believe men who are struggling with sexual addiction are good men who are unaware of the dynamics within themselves that they are playing out with the women in their lives*). When a woman is fully "selfed" (*Look at D.W. Winnocot's idea of "**True Self**"*), she is a deepening threat to the addict's self-preservation and the self-doubting man will either back away from her or potentially lash out in violence at her after his initial attempts of wooing go unanswered. Once the addict's shame is activated after a perceived "rejection", the typical response will be fight, flight or freeze. This will look like a combination of venom towards self (Self-Contempt), contempt projected outward (Other-Centered Contempt) and/or a relapse into their sexually compulsive behaviors to help self-soothe their narcissistic wounding.

Much of what the sexual addict masks are his deep insecurities and doubts about his own masculinity. Porn, for example, gives him that quick fix of affirmation that he needs to continue in his façade and feel the simultaneous power and powerlessness he so desperately longs for. (*Many addicts like the feeling of being in control and controlled at the same time.*) This also reinforces the duality of living a secret sexual life vs. being the man he pretends to be in the public arena.

Sexually compulsive behaviors can be used to cover a multitude of uncertainties within a man and can easily become a retreat from all things problematic. This place of reprieve from pain can feel like going to church. A sanctuary of addiction becomes a place of safety, worship, idolatry, and glorious gluttony. In this place of adoration, no one has permission to join in the addict's sacred space of ritualized reverence.

The non-addicted partner then longs even more for connection and genuine intimacy and will pursue the addicted one again and again. This constant search for genuine intimacy with the addict supports this "I love you & I hate you" dynamic. The internal dialogue within the addict goes something like this, *"I want you, Woman, because I am lonely and need people in my life, but I have no idea what to do with you when you are near, and you threaten the goodness of my dependence, so please go away."* I love you and I hate you. This *"push, pull"*, "come here, go away" posture can be maddening for the partner who loves her addicted spouse, yet as her husband's sexual dependency grows, she will feel more and more like she can no longer connect to him emotionally. This is because sexual addiction pulls the user out of his body. He becomes more and more disconnected from his true self and more outside of his own being, watching himself live. To be embodied while using pornography would be problematic because we are participating in objectification; we must detach from reality so our experience can be more gratifying. The core of addiction is escape, escaping our own body is primary to the addictive process. Would I truly enjoy orgasm if I allowed myself to believe that my porn usage leads to acts of misogyny and to dehumanizing sexual behavior and non-positive views of women? (Bridges, 2010) No way! I want to lie to myself as much as I can, so I continue to rest in the prison of my compulsions.

A Word to the Non-Addicted Partner

As the non-addicted partner navigates the many conflicting emotions she must continue to offer her truth and holy desire to her partner. To continually bring the fullness of her voice and her fear. "Where are you?", "I am having a hard time finding you.", "I miss connecting with you.", "Are you using pornography again?", "Will you get help?", "I am lonely and not okay, can we get help?" These are all fitting questions as she makes an effort to locate her lost partner. With bringing her true self to her partner he will be forced to face his own false self. With consistent boundaries, setting higher standards of fidelity within the relationship, and continued focus on improving her relationship with herself, the hope is that she can help create an environment where addiction does not flourish.

Let me make one point abundantly clear: **it is not the woman's responsibility to be an accountability partner or the sole support of the addict. He is solely responsible for his own integrity or lack thereof. She must require truth and open authentic engagement, but ultimately it is up to him what type of sexuality he will have.**

Much of the work of the non-addicted partner is that of differentiation and creating boundaries, rather than enabling the dysfunction to continue while in relationship, or turning a blind eye in willful ignorance. Support and love for the addict looks a lot more like holding your hand out rather than jumping into the raging river to attempt to save them from themselves.

It's important for the non-addicted partner not to take on what it is not theirs, hence the vital importance of differentiation. Sexual addiction is not a personal attack against who you are or the goodness of your body. It's not because something is wrong with your body or that your body is not "good enough". Your partner is going elsewhere to fulfill his desires because he is addicted and typically has been for decades, and this high consumption of porn has literally caused brain damage. As the non-addicted partner you'll have to discern between a personal betrayal of your sexual commitment and the belief that something is deficient within yourself (though many times the addicts in denial may want to project that onto you). Sex addicts have mastered the ability to sabotage genuine intimacy and shift responsibility away from themselves. It's most likely not your fault that you and your addicted partner are having troubles emotionally connecting; isolation is at the very core of all addiction.

As addicts, who we want to be is seldom who we are. If we allow someone to get close enough to us we will be exposed for the frauds that we truly are, so we isolate, hide from truth, and sabotage intimacy at all cost. I remember when my wife, Christy and I were just beginning to get more serious about our relationship. As it looked more and more like we were heading toward marriage, I freaked out and sabotaged our relationship. I was unfaithful to what we were feeling towards each other and instead of owning that fear and being truthful with my anxiety, I pulled away, acted childishly, and tried to get her to leave me first, so I didn't have to be the "bad guy". I was a coward. I knew she was a real woman, and I was not quite ready to be a real man. I felt like a boy inside, and the fullness of her womanhood terrified me and heightened all of my unaddressed insecurities. I finally came to the point of surrendering to the greater good despite my fear, but it took many painful come-to-Jesus moments to get to there. I actually loved Christy and knew I wanted to be with her, despite my fear that I could harm her and that I was not ready for genuine intimacy. Those first few years of marriage were very difficult, yet I am so proud of both of us for leaning into that discomfort rather than continuing to run from it.

For us addicts, we must lean into our ambivalent relationship with women. As we lean in, we will continue to learn to hold delight, bear beauty appropriately, and be able to attain a healthy committed sexuality. The work ahead for both sexual addicts and their non-addicted partners is similar and yet distinctly difficult. Each must continue to tell themselves the truth of their condition/enabling behaviors and radically embrace the goodness of who they are and what they are meant for.

Reference

Bridges, A. J. (2010). Pornography's effects on interpersonal relationships. *The Social Costs of Pornography: A Collection of Papers*, 89-110

DEAR OBJECTIFIED WOMAN

This letter will give words to what is happening inside an addicted man's mind. Misogyny is the hatred of women. Women suffer from the effects of misogyny daily because of men's unaddressed sexual brokenness. Here is a poem from an honest misogynist. I try to describe what is going through a man's psyche as he unconsciously uses a woman to mend his own wounded heart.

*Trigger warning for those women who have been objectified and abused. This is articulated in such a way to help a man identify his abusive style of relating, and is not meant in anyway to minimize a victims experience.

Dear Objectified Woman,

I like you. I really do.

But I like you more for what you can do for me, than for who you are.

You make me feel like a man, like I am funny; the king of the world.

Thank you for masking my insecurities, my immaturities.

I know how to make you feel good too. To make you feel beautiful, cherished, the only one. I know what you want. But I unconsciously only want you, as long as I can use you.

I need you to fill my sexual and emotional deficits, and until I get those wounds healed, I will continue to keep you close in my back pocket.

I can not risk being alone with myself. Because I (much like you) hate myself. I feel death when I have to face the man I am, and the man I am not.

I will choose cowardice.

I will hide behind you and continue to project my insecurities and fears onto your back; for it is the only way I know how to survive.

I need you to love me in the place my mother did not, my heart.

But I am terrified of the love I desire, so much so that I will do violence to you if you even try to come close. I want you to know my intentions are actually quite good, I don't want to do you harm, nor do I even know I am using you inappropriately.

I just feel my needs first; I am not concerned with yours. You are a means to an internal end.

I both despise myself for that and yet know of no other way.

From,

An honest misogynist

A MESSAGE TO MEN:
SEXUAL ABUSE, POWER & MISOGYNY

Another bombshell revelation in the news past month: Harvey Weinstein has used his place of power and influence to use and abuse a countless number of women. The response has been powerful with millions of women sharing their heartbreaking courageous stories on social media with a #METOO campaign shining light on the epidemic of male violence and sexual assault.

Harvey Weinstein follows others recently in the news as well: Bill Cosby, Donald Trump, Roger Ailes, Bill O'Reilly, Uber, NFL, and more stories emerging about the abuse of power within Catholic Church. Though this revelation is a shock to many, the 67% of women who have been physically or sexually abused in our society are not surprised at all.

You don't have to be an overt sexist to be part of the problem. As men, we have been socialized since we were very young that women were less than. Tony Porter in his powerful Ted talk "A Call to Men" says,

See collectively, we as men are taught to have less value in women, to view them as property and the objects of men. We see that as an equation that equals violence against women. We as men, good men, the large majority of men, we operate on the foundation of this whole collective socialization. We kind of see ourselves separate, but we're very much a part of it. You see, we have to come to understand that less value, property, and objectification is the foundation and the violence can't happen without it. So we're very much a part of the solution as well as the problem. The center for disease control says that men's violence against women is at epidemic proportions, is the number one health concern for women in this country and abroad.

As men, we must own our misogyny and our violence towards women and begin to change the heartbreaking all too common narrative. Silence is not okay! This is a man's issue and we must first address the violence within ourselves before we fix what is broken elsewhere.

Sadly, it's normally those who have been most harmed, impacted, and abused by men who are the ones who've had the courage to speak out against it. As men we have had the privilege to be blind to our own abuses against women as we have been living in the "Male box" (*society's unconscious blind blessing of misogyny*) or as Tony Porter calls it the "Man Box."

Feminists' and women's rights advocates' long-standing perseverance and moral outrage have called us to more, as the Greek biographer Plutarch once said, "Perseverance is more prevailing than violence; and many things which cannot be overcome when they are together, yield themselves up when taken little by little." For years women have been leading us and teaching us how to address our own violence, yet the many courageous women I know are tired of fighting a man's battle that ultimately must be addressed within ourselves. Those of us with privilege and power must pick up what moral indignation we have long left behind and stand up to other men when this sad cultural norm comes sauntering into our lives. (Look up Jackson Katz *"Bystander Approach"*)

Men are at a crossroads and must take ownership of their own violence against women and against each other.

Men who have not addressed their own issues of violence and abuse will surely continue it, intentionally or unintentionally. Tragically, throughout history, the behavior of Harvey Weinstein and many other men in power has been more the norm than the exception. While men may not be actively sexually harassing or assaulting women, through ignorance and silence, they enable such to continue. Turning the tide from power and control to one of equality and mutual respect will take all of us.

SEXUAL ADDICTION, MISOGYNY AND THE CHURCH

The Barna group launched a nationwide study on pornography called the "Porn Phenomenon." They report "most pastors (57%) and youth pastors (64%) admit they have struggled with porn, either currently or in the past." Though 56% of women under the age of 25 seek out pornographic materials, 81% of teen and young adult men have sought it out.[1] Further research suggests that this addicted male majority has unconsciously furthered systems of patriarchy, which advance pornographic styles of relating that reduce women to objects that could be mastered and controlled.[2, 3, 4]

Shame & Silence

The church is a notorious culprit of using shame and silence to restrict conversations around healthy sexual development. I believe this deafening silence is directly connected to the statistics above. The shame of hidden pornography use serves the purpose of keeping the addicted male leadership seeking control and setting up structures of power to hide behind. Of course, this is not true of all men in power; it's actually quite difficult to be in any management position, and even more difficult leading a church. This essay aims to name the ways the epidemic of pornography use within Christendom has led to unconscious misogyny within the Church and within American culture. My hope is to inspire the Church and those of us in positions of power to own our sexual brokenness and begin to lead our congregations from places of honor and equity instead of objectification and subjugation.

To transform these heartbreaking cultural norms as Christians we must lead with our brokenness, as Paul demonstrates in 1 Timothy 1:15 when he says, "Christ Jesus came into the world to save sinners, of whom I am the worst." Owning our sin involves confessing our sexual brokenness (including but not limited to pornography addiction). When we don't take ownership of our sexual brokenness, then our unacknowledged shame can have power over us. In men, for instance, this could lead many in leadership roles to restrict women to their "proper" place to lead the children's department and women's ministry, not allowing women in the pulpit or too close to the male leadership in unconscious fear of their sin being exposed. It is less about a woman's capability and more about the male leader's own intensifying of shame around his history of objectifying the feminine. I am aware, of course, this is not always the case with excluding women from leadership roles. There are many different theological positions, and if you hold these more classical positions I am not saying you are therefore addicted to pornography. I am saying, however, that there is a link between the degradation of women and the Church's silent complicity.

Power Dynamic

I know this dynamic worked well for my own sexual addiction when I was a pastor. I am sure I am not the only man who found their worth and security in positions of power, which a sexual addiction only affirmed. Power and pornography have a very interdependent relationship.[4] In regard to power, whoever is in charge gets to set the rules. When you have the power to define the "norms", you can make sure that they benefit you or those most like you. This is not a consciously selfish act; I have found most men have holy intentions, they just look out of the window of their own experience without taking the time to name their own implicit bias. They then define what is universally true for all, when it is actually only true for that person and those like him—rather than taking the time to listen to the experiences of different, diverse members of the body. This abuse of power comes from unaware privilege. The reality is that as a straight, white, Christian man, I must acknowledge and be aware that addiction influences my judgment and my leadership.

When this power dynamic is mixed with underlying sexual addictions it creates a perfect storm of an epidemic of church-ordained misogyny. Women are silenced, told to remain small, not to use their voice or their power. I believe this patriarchy-addicted system in the Church is insidious and will take men who have power to begin to break this wicked oppression of women. This is why we are seeing a record amount of women begin to come forward with their heartbreaking stories of sexual abuse, assault and harassment by men in power with the recent viral hashtag #MeToo. Christian men must listen, Christian men must humble themselves and respond with #BecauseofMe, owning our failures and toxic masculinity that has led to a posture of devouring rather than of honor towards the beauty and goodness of women. Men, this is our burden to bear and sadly we have been cowards.

All of Christ's bride must rise in defiance to this degrading attack of the Imago Dei in both the masculine and the feminine. Dehumanizing discourse against women can no longer be acceptable, and men must be man enough to say so. In particular, my call to men is that we use our privilege and power to stand up to injustice of all forms, including subversive forms of racism and sexism, and join alongside those who have been historically marginalized. By silencing a part of God's image in women, we are missing out on hearing from the very God who never stops speaking to us and through us all.

References

1) The Porn Phenomenon. (2016, June 19). Retrieved February 06, 2017, from http://www.barna.com/the-porn-phenomenon/#.VqZoN_krIdU

2) Bridges, A. J., Wosnitzer, R., Scharrer, E., Chyng, S., and Liberman, R. (2010). Aggression and Sexual Behavior in Best Selling Pornography Videos: A Content Analysis Update. Violence Against Women 16, 10: 1065–1085.

3) Boeringer, S. B. (1994). Pornography and Sexual Aggression: Associations of Violent and Nonviolent Depictions with Rape and Rape Proclivity. Deviant Behavior 15, 3: 289–304; Check, J. and Guloien, T. (1989). Repeated

Exposure to Sexually Violent Pornography, Nonviolent Dehumanizing Pornography, and Erotica. In D. Zillmann and J. Bryant (Eds.) Pornography: Research Advances and Policy Considerations (pp. 159–84). Hillsdale, N.J.: Lawrence Erlbaum Associates; Marshall, W. L. (1988). e Use of Sexually Explicit Stimuli by Rapists, Child Molesters, and Non-O enders. Journal of Sex Research 25, 2: 267–88.

4) Hald, G. M., Malamuth, N. M., and Yuen, C. (2010). Pornography and Attitudes Supporting Violence Against Women: Revisiting the Relationship in Nonexperimental Studies. Aggression and Behavior 36, 1: 14–20; Berkel, L. A., Vandiver, B. J., and Bahner, A. D. (2004). Gender Role Attitudes, Religion, and Spirituality as Predictors of Domestic Violence Attitudes in White College Students. Journal of College Student Development 45:119–131;

Zillmann, D. (2004). Pornogra e. In R. Mangold, P. Vorderer, and G. Bente (Eds.) Lehrbuch der Medienpsychologie (pp.565–85). Gottingen, Germany: Hogrefe Verlag;

Zillmann, D. (1989). E ects of Prolonged Consumption of Pornography. In D. Zillmann and J. Bryant (Eds.) Pornography: Research Advances and Policy Considerations (p. 155). Hillsdale, N.J.: L. Erlbaum Associates.

5) Smith, G. A., & Martínez, J. (2016, November 09). How the faithful voted: A preliminary 2016 analysis. Retrieved January 24, 2017,

from http://www.pewresearch.org/fact-tank/2016/11/09/how-the-faithful-voted-a-preliminary-2016-analysis/

6) Fahrenthold, D. A. (2016, October 08). Trump recorded having extremely lewd conversation about women in 2005. Retrieved February 21, 2017, from https://www.washingtonpost.com/politics/trump-recorded-having-extremely-lewd-conversation-about-women-in-2005/2016/10/07/3b9ce776-8cb4-11e6-bf8a-3d26847eeed4_story.html?utm_term=.2c0402766907

SPIRITUALITY

THE IDOLATRY OF SEXUAL ADDICTION:
WHEN SEX IS GOD & GOD IS SEX

The idea of idolatry rarely comes up when working through sexual addiction recovery, yet it seems to me one of the most important dynamics to engage when attempting to unwind the tangles of compulsive sexual behaviors. Sexual addiction can be a loaded term which is highly debated within the field of psychology; yet I know for my healing journey the naming and owning of my own sexual dysfunction/addiction was the beginning of becoming a more sexually healthy man. This revolution of healing transformation within my own body is the hope I hold for those I work with.

So why choose such a loaded term as idolatry? It is a weighty word that is often associated with shaming non-compliers into worshiping God more dutifully or to bang people over the head with scripture verses and searing guilt. I use this term "idolatry" to simply mean "a God-replacement". The idolatry of sexual addiction takes the most important seat in our lives and resides on the throne of our hearts; unexamined, it surreptitiously replaces the voice of the Spirit. Our internal thoughts are consumed with taking in what feeds our pornified pangs of hunger and we unconsciously scan our world to sexualize all heavenly delight and goodness. *(As addicts we cannot bear goodness well, so we sexualize it as a way to more easily digest.)* When sexuality becomes god it is impossible to attain the healthy meaningful sexuality that so many of us long to attain, yet don't quite know how to achieve.

How do you know if you are caught up in the idolatry of sexual addiction?

How much of your life is consumed by sexuality? In mutually nourishing intimate relationships, life is approached with rich balance. Sexuality is a very normal piece of the pie (SEE GRAPH). How much of your life does sexuality take up?

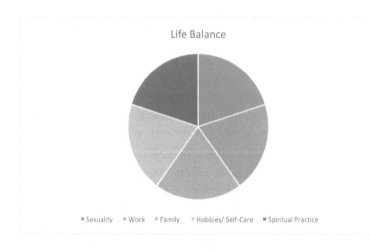

Life Balance

■ Sexuality ■ Work ■ Family ■ Hobbies/ Self-Care ■ Spiritual Practice

This will tell you if you have a problem with the idolatry of sexual addiction. There should not be a preoccupation with sex, but rather a well-adjusted delight in the sacred. Sexuality should be part of a larger style of life that is life-giving and self-affirming.

Another way to tell if this is a problem with idolatry for you or those you work with would be in regards to style of relating; do you or someone you work with have a pornographic style of relating? Or, as you look back at your past failed relationships, how did they end? Did it feel like the complete death of self? Did it feel like your entire world was crumbling through your fingertips? If so, you most likely were not only emotional enmeshed with your partner, but you were also likely caught up in the idolatry of that partner.

How do we dethrone this false God of sexual addiction?

We first must acknowledge that ***what you worship is what controls you.*** In other words, whatever you place your faith in is what masters you. Sexual addiction demands absolute governance and compliance. The compulsion occupies every edge of your being and manipulates behaviors and rules much in the same way a god would. Spiritually and sexuality are forever conjoined, so it's easy to complicate their union and forget which goes where in our lives.

This leads into my next point of reclaiming a healthier relationship with your sexuality, we must ***restore beauty, desire, & pleasure within sexuality as good and holy.*** As Balswick & Balswick (2008) state in their book *Authentic Human Sexuality: An Integrated Christian Approach*, "Unless our theology affirms the goodness of desire, we will be reluctant to integrate sexuality with spirituality. Desiring, enjoying and relating to a partner who is made in God's image affirms the sacred meaning embedded in the sexual union. Our desire can lead us to profound places of growth, for it takes courage to open ourselves, recognize in our quest for wholeness."

This integrative posture of sex & spirit is seen clearly in the category of beauty within pornography. Pornography can feel like the closest thing to heaven we can access. Beauty ignites our deepest arousal because beauty is what we are most made for. Do you bless the beauty and sweet desire of your sexuality? Or do you hold your sexuality and body in contempt? The profound goodness of your sexuality is meant to bring to life and joy, it is time for you endorse that fact. The more we bless our sexuality, the less power it has to rule us. Sex is so voraciously beautiful and so unapologetically pleasurable that even sexual idolization feels somewhat right. Yet something about acting out of compulsive sexual behaviors also feels so wrong. The intimacy promised in sexual addiction is never quite what is delivered.

To dethrone sexual addiction from dominion we must reclaim sexuality as a divine, infinite act of worship. It is no longer a cheap fix to satisfy a craving, but a prayerful sacred act of authentic love. Whether you are pleasuring your own body or that of a committed partner, you must honor and revere this beauty and pleasure rather than attempt to devour, consume and hoard. Pleasure is something to be fully present and responsible with, and not held with clumsy hands and shame. The addict tries to make pleasure his prisoner and stockpile it in an effort to reproduce it, not realizing genuine pleasure is not something that can be manufactured or fabricated, but found only in a loving relationship with a committed partner.

And finally, you must get help from a committed sage who knows both the darkness and the goodness of his or her own sexuality. The church has historically failed to create resources that are not shame driven or create a positive environment for healthy sexuality to emerge. Consequently, many folks have been made to search elsewhere to heal from this idolatry.

A Certified Sex Addiction Therapists (CSAT) can be incredibly helpful in addressing the addiction, but after the addiction is attended to and continually engaged, you must be steadfast in the pursuit of rebuilding a new sexuality that is not built on pornification. Other resources include the work of Dr. Patrick Carnes, Dr. Tina Sellers' new book on shame, sexuality, and the conservative church which is stellar, and she also leads intimacy retreats for couples who are looking to have a more robust sex life. As you are rebuilding your sexuality seeing an AASECT certified therapist would be valuable during this reconstruction phase.

LIVING IN TRUTH

L iving in truth means embracing a life of continual re-birth. It means bringing what is hidden into the light, exchanging the inauthentic for the genuine, and unearthing truths that have been underground for years. Yet the truth is difficult to confront. At times, it feels like the price of living into truth outweighs the expense of fabrication.

I remember Craig, a client who would not tell his wife about his early infidelities some fifteen years prior to their marriage. "But we are finally in a good spot," he said. As I asked him about his thinking regarding hiding this truth from his wife, he said he felt that the cost of truth was too high, that disclosing mistakes made when he was young might cause him to lose the woman to whom he was now fully committed. I told him that as I have grown and matured in my faith, I have found the opposite to be true. Living a hidden life always costs far more than living authentically; maybe not in the short term, but in the long tenure of life. Buddhist nun Pema Chodron says, "The essence of bravery is being without self-deception." The courage it takes to face ourselves as we are and tell the truth about what we see is worth significantly more than the heartache that will come of it. Now, I am not saying we must disclose everything in descriptive detail, as that could bring unnecessary pain to those we love. I am saying we can no longer hide, and masking the shadow parts of ourselves does not lead to a resurrected life, but a dead one.

If Craig had told the truth of his betrayal to his wife, he may have lost her. But what was the cost of his silence?

Because of his secrets, the very essence of intimacy with his wife was forfeited. Truth is at the core of all deep and genuine connection. Without resurrection truth breathing new life into our relationships, intimacy becomes stagnant and begins to perish. If Craig chose to remain silent and hidden, his marriage would surely die, for even if he stayed married, intimacy would not survive. When truth is avoided, the intimacy we seek—which is built on trust—will slowly decay, and more and more emotional detachment will create a distance that ensures the withering, if not the death, of our intimate relationships.

To tell the truth to his wife would feel like a death to Craig. While it very well might have meant the loss of his marriage, it is equally true to say that it would be the only way to save it. Truth eventually births new life, even if it initially looks like ruin. Craig chose to continue to keep secrets from his wife, and eventually quit therapy. He just wasn't ready to let go of what brought him so much safety and pleasure, but the cost will be high and the fall will be painful.

Many religious environments sell perfection as a form of redemption. This lie says that if you obey all the rules and are dutiful enough, faithful enough, and believe unquestioningly, you can attain perfect communion with God. The result is a church culture that, unconsciously or not, encourages hiding under the guise of spiritual "maturity."

I saw this dynamic play out in a conservative college I briefly attended. This particular institution had a spiritual "points" system: if you went to daily chapel services, church on Sundays, prayer meetings during the week, and on-campus Bible studies, you could earn the points that were required each semester. My 40 spiritual points didn't quite add up to the required 300, and I nearly flunked out before leaving of my own accord. Some 8 years after leaving that school I heard that my New Testament professor was caught cross-dressing and my Hebrew professor had an affair with his daughter's friend. I don't tell you this to somehow celebrate their pain or even judge their actions, but to demonstrate that truly living up to superficial standards of perfection is an impossible task. If we have no safe place to bring our real struggles, doubts, and heartache, we are likely to stray further from the truth and deeper underground with our pain.

(This essay is from my book published by NavPress: Stumbling Towards Wholeness: How the Love of God Changes Us)

SEX 101:
FOR PARENT'S & CHURCH LEADERS

"Our sexuality affects everything we do, and everything affects our sexuality. The same is true of our spirituality — that which is most deeply meaningful to us. We can deny both. But denying them does not mean they are not both alive in every breath and heartbeat of life."

— Tina Schermer Sellers, Sex, God, and the Conservative Church

Growing up in a more traditional church I was taught that sex was bad, dirty, and dangerous. The underlying message was "stay far, far, away from it, until you are married, then it's okay". There were no conversations about sex that were positive; sex was fire and if you got too close you would get burned. Period. *(If you want to know more about Shame & the Conservative Church please read Tina Sellers new book Sex, God, and the Conservative Church: Erasing Shame from Sexual Intimacy.)*

This "sex is bad" message that I received only made me want it more. The thrill of rebellion and the untouchability made me want to explore the "forbidden fruit" I was missing out on. So with only the word "no" and no further instructions or guidelines, I began my exploration.

My explorative journey was innocent at first. Then, with more seasoned friends showing me the way, I began to feel more confident and free to indulge. Pornography taught me how to relate to and engage with women, and slowly I became seductive and over-sexed. My interactions with women became potential places of fantasy fulfillment. Pornography taught me that anything was possible; I could let my lust run wild. You never know; the barista at the coffee shop could suddenly rip off her clothes and jump over the counter because she could not resist my bearded disposition! I had to be ready at all times! Clearly, this belief and others like it are absurd; the product of a pornified mind. We must address our unconscious beliefs about sexuality, so that we may transform them. Below is a helpful guide that we as parents and church leaders can follow to begin promoting healthy sexuality from our positions of power and influence.

What Can Parents & Church Leaders Do?

#1: Be Real About Sexuality

Our unaddressed sexuality comes out and impacts the way we lead and parent. With healthy sexuality in place, we can lead and parent from authenticity, which is what people, especially little people, need the most.

Yesterday we were all riding in our van from our family trip to Goodwill as we began discussing the beauty of how our bodies work. My four old loudly proclaimed "Women poop and pee from their vaginas!", and my two-year-old quickly retorted that "I pee from my penis!" Their shameless excitement for having figured out some new knowledge was palpable! Clearly, we had some clarifying to do, and we did. But I was so proud of my kids and frankly proud of us as parents that my kids are thinking and talking about their bodies (without shame!) and coming to us with their questions. As Tina Sellers always says, we must have 1,000's of small talks about sexuality with our kids, rather than the one big awkward "birds and the bees" talk. This practice sets a foundation for later in life, that sexuality and our bodies are not bad, but beautiful, and that it is safe to ask questions and talk about sex within our home, rather than to look to pornography or elsewhere for an education. Let's be real about our sexuality and break the cycles of silence and shame.

#2 Shame as Motivator

If our motivation is to help young people attain healthy sexuality and we attempt to do so by shaming them into health, we have a long way to go. Shame is a terrible motivator. Shame drives people into awful patterns of unhealthy sexuality and misplaced passions. Shame pushes sexuality underground, when it really needs to be exposed into a glorious light. Sex is fabulous and beautiful and we leaders must have the courage to enter into its terror and beauty with more integrity, nuance, and wisdom. Healthy sexuality and beauty are the best motivators to grow into mature sexual beings.

#3: The Moral Conversation Is Not Enough

The moral conversation was ultimately a shaming conversation. Let's take pornography, for example. The moral argument for looking or not looking at pornography was not motivating or powerful enough to actually promote lasting change, or to remove the desire not to objectify women. I knew looking at pornography was wrong, but could not stop until I grew a deeper understanding than just "don't do it because it's wrong." I needed to know the depths of women's goodness, I needed to know more deeply the depths of my own goodness.

The moral argument merely produces shame, which drives those who are struggling into compulsive sexual behavior to seek comfort and relief. As Robert Masters says in his brilliant book To Be A Man, *"The point is not to get morally righteous about this- for doing so only drives it further into the dark, and probably increases its appeal-but to look deeply enough into it to see its psychological, emotional, and social underpinnings."* Morality can never be the only conversation; a healthy and beautiful alternative must be offered.

#4: A Healthy Sexuality Must Be Offered

Though we did not talk about sex growing up, we all experienced it. As sexual beings, we cannot escape our sexuality. No matter how uncomfortable it was for our parents and/or our church leaders, their avoidance of this topic could not lessen its impact. Silence only served to hide our sexuality. Why are we freighted by something so glorious? Why so terrified of our own pleasure? We must begin to build and promote a new healthy framework around sexuality that our kids and our congregations are drawn to that is "sex positive" and affirms sex's beauty and honors its power. For this to happen we must be deeply in touch with our own personal narrative of sexuality. Without this connection, we will be cut off from our sexuality, thus not talking about it as often as we should.

#5: We Must Know our Own Story: *Holding our Sexual Brokenness and Goodness Close*

Have you told the truth about your life? If it's true that "our sexuality mirrors everything else we do in our life" (Masters 2015), we must be honest with our sexual stories. Have you been sexually abused? Have you been a sexual abuser? Have you been shamed for your beautiful body? What is your story of sexuality? Have you spent your time and energy minimizing your own darkness and sexual brokenness or degree of compulsive sexual behaviors? Have you made your sexuality all about darkness and brokenness? We have to make peace with our stories of sexuality, both in their glory and depravity. We must tell the truth of our sexual complexities. Many folks either deny their sexual brokenness or indulge in it; neither are healthy. Many people ignore the beauty and deep goodness of their sexuality, and thus remain disconnected from a core part of what makes them most human.

Brokenness

We must own our sin and sexual brokenness regularly. As Christians we must lead with our brokenness to transform the depraved cultural norms, as Paul demonstrates in 1 Timothy 1:15 *"Christ Jesus came into the world to save sinners, of whom I am the worst."*

I facilitated a workshop on addiction a few years ago. The workshop was nearing a close, and I was fielding questions from the audience. I was asked a question along the lines of: "Have you as a professional ever struggled with your own addictions?" I was presented with an opportunity to break my silence—to step out of hiding for the first time with people I sensed would embrace me in the midst of my shame. I knew from my experience with clients who had honored me with their shame stories that inviting a safe person into the places where self-condemnation prevailed was liberating and healing. With trepidation but hope, I admitted to a room full of strangers that I had been addicted to Internet pornography. I had never confessed my addiction out loud, except within the confines of therapy. When the words left my lips, I nearly lifted my hands in an attempt to grab them and wrangle them back into my mouth. Panic-stricken, I thought to myself, *what have I done?* But then I began to feel something wash over me; a divine and holy kindness, like baptismal waters washing away my shame. Maybe that is what the Holy Spirit feels like. In a place where I had always held self-contempt, kindness snuck in. The shame lifted as I entered my brokenness, and I was able to own my story publically for the first time.

As I gazed around the room, scanning for expressions of judgment and disgust, I found none. What I did find were soft eyes full of tears and kindness locked onto mine; their faces were gentle, their bodies leaning in toward mine as I continued to share briefly about my addiction journey. Even though I had spent years in therapy engaging my shame and experiencing a modicum of healing, this terrifyingly sacred experience of self-disclosure turned out to be the most liberating of all, not only for me but perhaps even for my listeners. Marianne Williamson wrote, "As we are liberated from our own fear, our presence automatically liberates others." I had been liberated from my fear, from my shame and self-hatred, and because of that freedom, others began to feel the same release. Many folks came up to me after the workshop and thanked me for my courage. Through continued acts of bravery into brokenness, we can be healed.

Goodness

Sexuality is not simply about brokenness. We can't only talk about the negative or painful aspects of our sexuality; we must possess the strength to enter into its glory and beauty. It's difficult for us to bear beauty well, we normally get spooked and sabotage it. Goodness feels too vulnerable and exposes core desires we may not have quite made peace with yet. That exposure is terrifying if someone else has access to our raw, open sexuality. Embracing sexual goodness produces hope and desire, which feel entirely too susceptible to heartbreak. So instead we cling to control, focus only on our brokenness, and become convinced that even if goodness exists, it surely won't last. What does it mean for you to press into the goodness of your sexuality? Ask yourself, why am I so negative in my approach to something so holy?

#7: Telling the Truth of our Stories:

We not only must **know** the truth of our stories but we also must **tell** the truth of our stories. Despite the potential darkness or fear of our stories, God is truth. The more we tell the truth of both our glory and our darkness, the more we can experience God. Men must humble themselves, own their failures, and make peace with their shame of being part of the suppressive system that has degraded half of God's image and oppressed women. Women must make peace with their shame and self-contempt. Women: it is not your fault or your body's fault if you were abused by an insecure and fragmented man who attempted to devour you. If men and women can begin to tell the truth of their experiences, true understanding and forgiveness will come as result. Here is a beautiful heart-wrenching example of telling the truth of sexuality, this is an example of brokenness, humility, courage, forgiveness, and reconciliation. Our story of rape and reconciliation Thordis Elva and Tom Stranger. (*Trigger warning to those who have been abused.*) When we tell the truth of our stories, we have the opportunity to break cycles that we have historically enacted.

HEALING

PRACTICAL STEPS FOR RECOVERY

Behavior modifications are helpful at the beginning of the process, but if this is where you stop engaging your relationship to porn, you will never have full liberation from it. To actually end your addiction, you must address the pain behind the porn. Your core wounds drive your addiction. Behavioral changes help get some distance from pornography so you can begin to feel shifts in your habits and increase clarity of thought.

Construct a Porn Free World:

This is the most difficult yet most important first step if you are serious about recovery. This is the stage where people get rid of their smart phones and trade for a flip phone, rid themselves of laptop computers, and disable many practical steps of their ritualized practice with porn. Study what you normally do; we all ritualize our porn use. Do you always use right before bed on your cell phone? Know your patterns and what you have ritualized. Put an end to it. Any place or item you have eroticized, you must change. Sabotage your ability to use. This is not forever. You can reintroduce technology later after you have changed your relationship to it, but right now having your smart phone laying next to your bed is automatically arousing. No person can consistently have enough self-control to say no when that amount of pleasure is literally right next to you 24 hours a day. Construct a porn free world which will give you the space from porn to begin to deal with the root of the problem: the core wounds that drive the addiction.

Go See a Counselor:

A good counselor can be hard to find. I tell people it's like dating. Most of the dates you go on will be pleasant but not the right fit. Continue to seek a wise sage who knows the depths of both heartache and joy; someone who is familiar with the snares of addiction yet not judgmental or shaming. Look for someone who has a positive, non-shaming view of sexuality and yet understands the dark side; that it can be used inappropriately to hide from our true selves. One place to look for a good therapist is the International Institute for Trauma & Addiction Professionals. https://www.iitap.com/therapists-search/. Another place to look is the www.AllenderCenter.org which specializes in sexual abuse and trauma.

Engage in Authentic Community:

There are many free group resources out there. SA (Sexaholics Anonymous), SAA (Sex Addicts Anonymous), SLAA (Sex and Love Addicts Anonymous); Celebrate Recovery is a Christian based program focusing on a variety of addictions, these are just a few of the more popular ones. Though each vary in the specifics of what is offered, the most important part is finding a group of people you can journey with who are experiencing a similar transformation. Here you will find much needed support, honesty, authenticity, and a place to practice coming out of hiding and living into true vulnerable relationship. Some of these groups may not be that helpful, don't lose heart, continue to seek out authentic community and people who are willing to look at the depths of their own darkness.

Pornography Recovery Materials:

It's important to regularly read and dive into recovery materials on a daily basis. Reading and watching resources adds tools to your tool belt to help you engage your addiction in a healthy way.

Books

The Porn Trap: The Essential Guide to Overcoming Problems Caused by Pornography, Wendy & Larry Maltz, 2009.

Your Brain on Porn and the Emerging Science of Addiction, Gary Wilson & Anthony Jack, 2014

Pornland: How Porn Hijacked Our Sexuality, Gail Dines, 2011 Beacon Press

Big Porn Inc. Exposing the Harms of the Global Pornography Industry, 2011, ed. by Melinda Tankard Reist & Abigail Bray

Unwanted 2018, Jay Stringer, NAVPRESS

Video Resources

"Porn on the Brain" Dr. Valerie Voon, UK Documentary
http://www.independent.co.uk/lifestyle/health-and-families/health-news/pornography-addiction-leads-to-same-brain-activity-as-alcoholism-ordrug-abuse-study-shows-8832708.html;

http://dailymail.co.uk/news/articl-2428861/Compulsivepornography-users-shows-brain-activity-alcoholics-drugs-addicts.html;

The Great porn experiment, Gary Wilson, Ted Talk,
https://www.youtube.com/watch?v=wSF82AwSDiU;

Why I stopped watching porn, Ran Gavrieli Ted Talk,
https://www.youtube.com/watch?v=gRJ_QfP2mhU

Websites

Culture Reframed- Research-driven education to prevent, resist, and heal the harms of violent mainstream pornography and hypersexualized pop culture. http://www.culturereframed.org/

Fight the New Drug http://www.fightthenewdrug.org/
Fortify- https://www.joinfortify.com/

Your Brain on Porn- http://www.yourbrainonporn.com
Enough is Enough- www.enough.org. Their mission is to make the Internet Safer for Children and Families.

1) Write your Story:

Assignment #1

In no less than 1,000 words, tell your story of sexuality. This should be a detailed time-line of your sexual development, a map to locate where you have been. Start at the beginning. How was sexuality introduced to you? How was sexuality talked about or not talked about in your home? What was the first time you were introduced to pornography? Sexual abuse? Begin to unpack your story.

Assignment #2

Choose one memory from assignment #1 and dive deep into that story. Use all five senses, in the scene of abuse, or first exposure to pornography, or sexual betrayal. What were the smells, the sights, what did the chair or bed feel like? What was the taste? During this assignment you are landing the plane into your story of sexuality, not merely flying over it. You must feel the weight of the story, if you are not feeling it or wanting to distance yourself from it, it is not worth your time doing it. Allow your body to enter back into what it has been trying to escape all these years.

Assignment #3

Repeat. What stories still bear shame? What stories do you still not talk of openly? Where do you still hide? Where your fear and your shame are is where you need to go next. Write, bleed, suffer into your words, this practice will help free you from addiction and create a depth and richness to your healing journey.

2) Live in Truth:

The truth about our sexuality can feel like a terrifying monster. The beast comes knocking on our door, hungry and ready to devour; he haunts and taunts our every move. Our response is to bar the door, nailing pieces of wood across the entrance, triple-bolt locking it, even pushing furniture up to the entry to block the colossus from overtaking us. After the door looks secure we run into the corner and cower with a variety of weapons in hand. We are truly terrified of our true sexuality, yet if faced with fear and timidity, the monster of our sexual addiction will never leave; its presence will only become more powerful. The more we attempt to hide from its presence, the more authority we give it.

What if we engaged the scary truth of our relationship to pornography differently? What if we invited through the door what we fear most? What if we confronted what is most true, yet equally most terrifying, about ourselves? What if we came to the door and told the monster it could come in for a brief conversation? We must be curious as to why the monster is there in the first place. "Why are you here?" we may ask. "What can I do for you?" Can we listen with inquisitiveness to the behemoths that most haunt us? We must if we are to be free of our fear and develop the healthy sexuality that we long for.

Does your monster have a face? A tone to its voice? After the conversation you can lead the monster back to the door, reassuring it that if it needs anything else it can come back for another conversation while also setting clear boundaries so the monster can never rule you by its tactics of fear and intimidation again. Cowardice can be a cruel master. Reclaiming your power over the monsters (your compulsive sexual behaviors) that haunt you is vital to stepping into healing.

THE DIFFERENTIATED SELF:
CREATING HEALTHY REALATIONSHIP

The term "*differentiation*" has recently come up in my own individual therapy as one of the core issues that I must address within myself. My hope is not only to discover what it means to be well differentiated, but why it's important for us to understand the complexities of this way of being.

As I reflect on my own life I remember situations where someone else's decision (whether good or bad) totally took me out. I'm talking about days of crying myself to sleep, weeks of disorientation and numbness, months of depression. This has happened within my own family relationships, interpersonal relationships, romantic relationships, and even organizational ones. I am realizing what Kerr and Bowen said nearly 30 years ago: "poorly differentiated persons tend to be more emotionally reactive" (p. 320) is completely true of me. Why do I allow other people's feelings, opinions, and decisions to have so much power over my own? How do I (and we) learn to be well differentiated? This isn't just an important question to answer, but a vital remedy to continuous patterns of heartbreak.

Skowron and Freidlander (1998) explain *"Differentiation of self is defined as the degree to which one is able to balance (a) emotional and intellectual functioning and (b) intimacy and autonomy in relationships (Bowen, 1978). On an intrapsychic level, differentiation refers to the ability to distinguish thoughts from feelings and to choose between being guided by one's intellect or one's emotions*" (Bowen, 1976, 1978). Basically, differentiation means a healthy separation of one's self.

When a rupture occurs within our thought life, we tend to immediately turn inward towards self-contempt or outward to blame and/or shared contempt (other-centered contempt) as an effort to get the dysfunction outside of ourselves as quickly as possible. Neither of these choices are helpful solutions to the core issue of emotional enmeshment and triangulation, thus we see the need for discovering how to attain healthy differentiation.

Emotional enmeshment and triangulation are subtle forms of abuse, and consequently more difficult to address because of their subversive nature. The easiest form of triangulation/enmeshment to recognize is that of Parent/Child/Parent (*Note: Emotional triangles can happen anywhere, read Edwin Friedman, A Failure of Nerve, Chapter 7, if you want a more in-depth reading on emotional triangles*). Dr. Allender also talks about triangulation in his new book, *Healing the Wounded Heart (*2016*)*, in referring to the origins of Parent/Child/Parent enmeshment he writes, "*It is a simple equation: to the extent there is a loss of intimacy, passion and purpose with one's spouse, the higher the probability a child will be used as a spousal replacement.*" We find ourselves lured into these triangulated relationships because we have a holy desire to be included, affirmed, and loved. At first, these relationships give life and the promise of hope fulfilled, but over time the emotional drainage serves to only take our very life away.

A helpful metaphor of differentiation is that of a raging river. Imagine a loved one is caught in the raging rapids. Maybe they are in the throngs of addiction, maybe just incredibly depressed or lonely, but either way, they are drowning. Of course, our first instinct is to jump in and rescue them, thinking that is what love looks like. But if you jump into the raging river, you too will surely be sucked into the torrent and swept away by the rapids. That is not love, but suicide. True love and proper differentiation is to stand on solid ground, with feet firmly planted on the water's edge, with your arm reaching out towards your loved one, allowing them to swim towards your hand when they are ready to receive the help they need.

So what do you do if you notice you are involved in an emotional enmeshed and triangulated relationship? We must not turn against ourselves or the other. Whether we initiated the unhealthy relationship or merely caught in the web of it, we must be gentle and kind to why we got into the relationship in the first place. Second, we must have the courage to name and address what needs to be changed within our own heart, and not focus on what we hope to change in the others involved. Why were you drawn to this type of relationship? What core needs are you attempting to meet by engaging in a triangulated dynamic? What does the quality of the relationship say about you?

Finally, we must reclaim a strong sense of self. Do you know who you are apart from the blessing or curse of another? Do you know your place in God's Kingdom? We must have a deeply anchored sense of who we are, rooted in who God has called us to be. If not, we can be seduced away by well-intentioned folks who unconsciously divert us so they can get their own emotional needs met.

Being well differentiated does not mean being emotionally closed off or cold hearted; quite the opposite. It means being so in touch with how you feel and why you feel it that you make the difficult choice of doing what is best for you. This is not a selfish act; knowing what emotions are yours to bear and which emotions are not a sign of emotionally maturity and growth

References

Bowen, M. (1976). Theory in the practice of psychotherapy. In P. J. Guerin, Jr. (Ed.), Family therapy: Theory and practice (pp. 42-90). New York: Garner Press.

Bowen, M. (1978). Family therapy in clinical practice. New York: Jason Aronson.

Skowron, E. A., & Friedlander, M. L. (1998). The Differentiation of Self Inventory: Development and initial validation. Journal of counseling psychology, 45(3), 235

THE PAIN BENEATH THE PORN:
GETTING TO THE ROOTS

Robert Masters writes in his phenomenal book "To Be a Man", "*What we do sexually is a reflection of what we're doing with the rest of our lives*". This statement is profoundly true, and so is its opposite. What we have done with our lives (or what has been done to us), is also a reflection of our sexuality. Meaning if we live fairly hidden, non-authentic lives, most likely we will be hidden and non-authentic with our sexuality. If you have a history of shame, what you do with your sexuality will reflect the shame you have lived. If you have experienced trauma and have not properly addressed/confronted the wreckage, the unprocessed pain will unconsciously guide how you live, this dynamic is called a reenactment. One way we reenact our unprocessed wounds is by sexualizing or erotizing them.

We sexualize our wounds in a desperate attempt to heal our unaddressed pain. Porn can help for a short time and temporarily meet many of the core needs (love, touch, emotional attunement, pleasure and delight) we may not have received as a child. For example, if your parents were emotionally distant, you probably longed for intimate connection. Though you were powerless to control what you received or did not receive from your parents when you were a child, as an adult you choose to have power and control over this deep unmet longing for intimacy by using pornography to attempt to tend to that core wound. It's important to note that your desire for intimacy is beautiful and good, and though your parents were not able to be provide enough of it, it was not your fault that you were drawn to a quick imitation. You were made for intimacy, of course, you were drawn to it wherever you could find it. But now that you have become an adult, you bear responsibility for what you choose to do with your sexuality and how you choose to engage it.

We must get to the pain beneath the porn and begin to heal what is driving the porn use in the first place. If your mother was smothering, this may have created in you a feeling of overwhelming powerlessness, maybe this led to you seeking out pornography that was male dominated, where the male in the scene had all the power and the women had none. When we can hold our sexuality and arousal without judgment it can be a map to guide us into deeper healing and liberation. Porn comes in and can initially slow the bleeding of the wound. But ultimately, it's a Band-Aid on a shotgun wound that does not heal the core injury. One common wound that is often neglected that I will speak about more fully here is the mother wound.

The Mother Wound

Our core woundedness can come in many shapes and sizes. There is no one size fits all when it comes to trauma. This mother wound can come in the message of "not enough". Not being held enough, or not being engaged in healthy, non-sexual touch as a child, or not feeling delighted in, or your emotional world not being tended to. The other extreme also creates the same wounding of "too much" intimacy. Maybe you were held and pursued too much, personal boundaries were constantly being infringed upon, leading to fear of being consumed by your mother. Both of these forms of triangulation with the mother can create an anxiety and woundedness that we seek porn to mend.

We must continue to push into our stories around our mothers to continue to dig out the roots of what drives our addictive tendencies and stop our unhealthy patterns of relating. Consider these questions as you try to kindly explore the origins of your and mother's relationship.

- Was she cold and emotionally distant?
- Was she emotionally cavernous?
- How did she relate to you emotionally, physically?
- Was she full of rage?
- Manipulation?
- Seduction?
- How did she get her emotional needs met?

Our mothers are the primary example of the feminine to us; how she engaged you taught you how to engage women. If you are still holding anger and resentment towards your mother (unaddressed wound) is it possible that unconsciously you have been trying to get back at your mother by objectifying women all these years?

We eroticize our deepest wounds not only as an attempt to heal but also as a way to make sense of our pain. (Read Robert Master's work if you want to know more about erotized wounds). How do our wounds of our mothers become eroticized? It's a simple equation of whatever core needs you are missing out in childhood you will unconsciously seek to fulfill in adolescence and adulthood, many times through pornography, as it's the easiest and most accessible. I also think it's quite unique how these wounds are played out with each person, yet the foundational longings remain the same; deep love, genuine intimacy, and authentic connection.

A few questions you might ask yourself as you are trying to look beneath your porn use.

- What type of porn most arouses you?

- What is desire beneath your porn?

- You are longing for genuine connection; is there a better way to find this desire than the ways you have tried

MASTURBATING WELL

It's a common question I get asked and a continuous debate within Christian circles: What about masturbation? Is it okay to masturbate, or not? If only it were that simple. The typical dialogue within the church of "yes or no" or "good vs. bad" lacks the maturity and nuance needed to discuss and understand this topic. Good Christian men and women are confused and wanting to please God. **What if pleasuring ourselves could actually bring pleasure to God?** Is that even possible? There is much to unlearn and relearn on how to masturbate well.

You may have grown up with an understanding of masturbation as the "forbidden fruit", or a sin just as reviled as murder. You may have heard myths of going blind or growing hair on your palms. Most likely you heard nothing at all. Silence. And the silence was enough for you to to learn to say nothing, but feel everything. This is the origin of searing shame. The shame becomes unbearable for those of us who want to please God, yet can't resist bringing ourselves pleasure. Instead of being shamed for wanting pleasure and enjoying pleasuring ourselves, we need to learn to masturbate in a healthy way.

Unlinking Porn & Masturbation

Many folks misuse masturbation. Some use it compulsively as form of escape, for others it is a way to dissociate from their present struggles and/or overwhelming joys. We must begin to unlink porn and masturbation in order to reclaim a better relationship with our sexuality; this can take time. Patterns of masturbation have been linked to objectification and fantasy which can be difficult to break. If you have engaged in the same rituals for the last two decades, it's probably safe to say you wouldn't be able to make these changes overnight. Masturbating differently will take significant work and effort on your part.

Fantasy Structures

While it can be simple to stop looking at erotic images on the internet, the hardest healing work is beginning to engage your fantasy structures and thought life. Christian folks call it "taking every thought captive", the world of psychology calls it "thought stopping". The sin is not in the act of masturbation but in the fantasy. Our thoughts can be perverse and laced with objectification, and this is the darkness that we must flee, not the act of masturbation itself. Can you masturbate without debasing fantasy? If not, then don't do it; you're not ready yet to reintroduce healthy masturbation into your life. There has to be a significant and consistent break from your use of porn and a rewiring of your brain and fantasy life. After time has passed, and you have worked hard to allow your brain time to heal, reworked your fantasy structures and how you honor women in your thought life, I believe you can reintroduce healthy masturbation within proper boundaries.

If you are single, you will have to be aware of the difference between healthy masturbation vs. the patterns of how you have engaged in the past. If you begin to pleasure yourself and find your brain drifting into fantasy, stop. If you find yourself using masturbation to run from emotion, stop. **Masturbation must be used to enhance reality not escape from it.** Within these guidelines, it will not be compulsive and will be less frequent because of the boundaries of health you have put in place.

Breaking Isolation

One reason masturbation can be such a tricky part of the healing process is that is so isolating. This aspect itself can be triggering. Part of breaking the cycle for folks who are married is beginning to be honest with your partner about your relationship to masturbation. Your sexuality is no longer solely your own; it is now shared. If you have gotten to the point of being able to masturbate well without fantasy and escape, you can incorporate it into your sexuality with your partner

WHY I AM INSECURE AND WANT MY WIFE TO PAY FOR IT

When you come from a broken home, broken feels like home. Chaos is the norm and normal feels like chaos. How do we fight back? Those of us who have made ourselves at home in dysfunction? I know for me, I have no idea, which is why I write: to try and unwind ways of being that no longer serve me.

One such way of being is my insecure defensive posture when I am confronted with any sort of critique, or anything that even smells a bit like it. My guard immediately goes up and I stop any form of impact from being made on me. This shows up most in my own marriage. The irony of marriage is that Christy (my wife) gets the very worst and the very best of who I am. The heights of heaven and the depths of hell all bound within one relationship.

There are times she will ask me, "Would you mind picking up your clothes?" or "Would you mind cleaning the kitchen?" and many times my default is to attack—not physically, but much worse, emotionally. "Well I did take out the trash, take the kids to school, make breakfast…" My justifications go on and on. I already have my guard up. I am unconsciously looking for a fight. Why? Why do I do that? I don't actually want to be mean to my wife, I like her (most days I really do), so why do I return to an immature way of being?

The simple answer is, I learned it. The more complex answer is that it continues to work for me. I learned it from my family of origin: recovering from my parents' divorce without any emotional processing, we turned on each other—survival of the meanest. I developed a sharp wit and a mean bite. It protected me, kept my heart safe from harm, and it still works for me. If I can defend and conceal my insecurity from my wife, then I won't feel exposed. One of the greatest fears for an insecure man is exposure of what we most want to hide and protect. (*This is also why so many insecure/immature men are involved in pornography*). We want to hide our futility, our powerlessness, and our young tender places within our souls. We unconsciously believe that if these places were exposed we would be less likely to be loved. Rather, the opposite is true: **the more we expose our innermost vulnerabilities in trusting relationship, the more others are drawn to our goodness and away from our addictions.**

This happens most in our most intimate relationships because we know that our partners see right through us, they know our truest self. My unconscious fear is being revealed to my wife who already comprehends my deepest insecurities. I choose to defend rather than have the courage to be vulnerable with her about my fears of not being enough, or not having what it takes to love her or be a good father. The sad irony of this process is that I defend most where I need love most. These vulnerable places inside of me are the very places that need tenderness, love, and deep care. What I find when I lean into those raw places is that I am actually more terrified to be loved well than I am to be alone. It is easier for me to push her away than receive her holy love for my tender places within.

So back to the how question. How do I (and maybe we) stop reenacting this insecure defensive way of being? A few steps come to mind:

Awareness & Vulnerability

A new awareness starts by asking yourself tough questions and beginning to tell yourself the truth of who you have become in light of your story. When I feel myself beginning to defend, I must stop and ask, "What am I defending right now? What am I scared of? Do I trust who I am with right now enough to show my heart instead of my anger?" If I can center myself back into what is true, I can begin to create a new way of being that is rooted in courage and vulnerability and not defensiveness and addiction.

Blessing

As I learn to let my defenses go, I first must bless the way my defenses have saved me and served me. I must bless my story. "Thank you, sharp wit and defensive posture, you have kept me safe from harm and injustice. I am now safe, and an adult, and no longer need you to protect me, as I can now protect myself." When we bless our insecurities and defense mechanisms, we can find the strength to release them.

Developing a New Way of Being

A new way of being must take the old one's place. You must practice this new centered, non-defensive posture with kindness and grace toward yourself. As Malcolm Gladwell says, it takes 10,000 hours of practice to become a professional at anything. It is no different with new ways of being; you spent your entire life living out of your old way, and it will take time for a new way of being to emerge.

As I become more aware, choose vulnerability, bless, and step into a new way of being, I can love with deeper hope and a richer courage. I know I will still fall into old patterns. I actually responded defensively again to my wife last night as I was reading aloud this essay on "overcoming my defensiveness..." Yet I am confident that as I have the bravery to name and bring my own sin to light, glory, goodness and liberation will soon follow.

Andrew J. Bauman is a therapist, writer and teacher who resides in Seattle, WA. He holds a Master of Arts in Counseling Psychology and is currently working on his Doctorate. The Psychology of Porn is his second published book. Andrew is married to Christy Bauman, and they have three beautiful children, Brave, Wilder, and Selah. You can follow his work and check out his other products at www.AndrewJBauman.com.

Made in United States
Troutdale, OR
11/04/2024